How to Stay
When You Want to Quit:
*A business parable for busy professionals
tired of whining*

Other Books By Karl Bimshas

Leadership Books
"Pushing Back the Ocean"
"How to Stay When You Want to Quit"
"How to Fix Your Whine at Work"
"Quick Ways to Be a Good Leader"
"Don't Be the A-Hole on The Team"
"Go Get It!"
"Leaders Don't Shrug"
"Give a Damn"

Leadership Essays
"So, I've Been Thinking"
"So, I've Been Thinking Some More"
"Think Again"
"An Unusual Year"

Fiction
"He Loves It When She Smiles"
"Three Blinks and a Sigh"
"More Pepper, Less Salt"

How to Stay
When You Want to Quit:
A business parable for busy professionals
tired of whining

KARL BIMSHAS

BimMedia
San Diego, California

Third Printing: 2023

www.KarlBimshasConsulting.com

ISBN: 978-1-312-48542-6

DEDICATION

For those at their wit's end.

TABLE OF CONTENTS

PREFACE

We often admire those who have said they've never worked a day in their life because they've loved their job. This book isn't for them. Besides, they're liars.

Most people have had a time in their life when they have wanted to quit their job, school, a relationship, or a volunteer committee but instead stayed. They found a way. They did not quit and it made all the difference.

Some people quit but never leave. This book isn't for them either. This book is for the persistent few, those with grit, stick-to-itiveness, and an inner passion yearning to be free. These people do not quit, period.

I lived much of this story; both the positive and the negative. My negative experience caused me to start business writing, a cathartic event that has led to far better things. After reading this parable, I'm confident you'll be led to do better things too.

This book is in your hands for one of several reasons:

1. Someone who cares about you thinks you've been a royal pain in the neck lately, and they believe the wisdom shared in this story may help you.

2. You're proactive and reading this in search of tips and clues before anyone calls you out on your recent lackluster behavior.

3. You've stumbled across a discarded copy from some poor soul who's not ready to hear hard truths.

Regardless of the reason, invest a few minutes in reading this short tale and extracting the tips and philosophies that work for you.

INTRODUCTION

This is a story about two friends, Max and Maddie, who are pressing hard in their careers. Maddie is fortunate to work with a great boss who has mentored and challenged her to be her best. Max has had the opposite experience. He has been through a heavy rotation of managers, many of whom spoke a good game but never really showed up to play. The most noticeable difference between them is that Maddie, although not yet in her ideal job, loves the journey, while Max is miserable on his voyage.

Read on to learn how Maddie takes what she has learned and helps Max turn his attitude and life around.

You'll pick up a few tips to bring positive action to people who are disillusioned in their current jobs, even if that person is you.

I first shared the main concepts in this story in a speech many years ago. Since then, the idea of not quitting has taken many forms, from personal tirades and lectures to several incarnations of prose. Settle in and enjoy this evolution from whiner to winner.

THIS JOB REALLY SUCKS

Clicking keyboard keys, chirping phones, the monotone sound of uninspired hushed voices, and all the other maddening sounds of general office din played outside Max Gray's office. He had arrived to work well-dressed but was now disheveled and had a bleak look around his eyes. He massaged his temples with his fingers to fight off a fresh headache. Papers, tattered file folders, binders, policy manuals, marketing plans, and aged corporate initiatives cluttered his office.

He rummaged through open browsers on his laptop, paused, and flipped through a nearby report with the tiresome tedium every office worker with a soul-crushing fluorescent light buzzing above their head experiences. A sliver of sunshine forced its way through the clouds and captured his attention. He stood up from his desk, meandered toward the window, and scanned the midmorning cityscape.

In the park below, young children played catch with an exuberant dog. He noticed an elderly couple with their arms linked, admiring a patch of flowers. With a reluctant smile, he turned to his desk and opened the top drawer to reveal a folder titled: "Change Plan Goals". He reached for it, but the booming voice of his boss startled him.

Fred Seaver was a middle-aged, gruff, unkempt man who clutched a water bottle by his side like an oxygen tank. He stuck his head past the doorway and into Max's office.

"I need you to get me the numbers for the tandem report before the end of the day," he said.

Max shoved the drawer shut as if caught peeking at something he wasn't supposed to. "Ahh, yeah, they should be done before

13

the…" Max's voice petered to a mumble when Mr. Seaver walked away, disinterested. Max paused, took a deep breath, and sighed in anguish. "This job really sucks."

His declaration hung in the air for a moment. A temporary self-satisfied look of relief crept across his face before it once again melted with the pang of torment. He picked up his cell phone and tapped a few numbers.

"How about lunch?" he asked.

Max sat in a booth with Maddie Tait, his friend of several years. Maddie was radiant, with an air of confidence and professionalism in stark contrast to Max's hunched posture.

"So your job isn't fun anymore?" she asked.

"Maddie, it's not only my job," Max said. "My weekends are no longer fun either. On Saturdays, I veg out all day, maybe do laundry or hit the grocery store, and by Sunday night, I'm filled with anxiety instead of anticipation. On Monday, every day really, I go back to my drab work routine." His eyes darted between the tabletop, Maddie, and the ceiling. "Sometimes, something catches my attention, and I daydream about beginning a new project, something better aligned with my personal goals. But trying to reconnect with why I wanted this job in the first place is pointless."

"Oh, sweetie," Maddie said, her head tilted empathetically.

"I used to want to make a difference, but things have changed," Max said. "I've been so busy sorting through all the corporate fire drills, paperwork, and bureaucracy, I didn't see what was happening around me."

"I know where this is going," Maddie said.

"I sensed it was happening, but I didn't want to admit it — until today. My job sucks, and I want to quit," Max said.

Maddie nodded as Max, wracked with anxiety, rolled the corners of his paper placemat.

"How are you sleeping," she asked. "You look tired."

"Sleep? What's that?" Max laughed. "At best, my nights are a series of fitful naps. By morning, I'm a grumpy basket case. I snap at people who cut me off on the way to work, and I'm frustrated because my coworkers don't seem to have any passion, either. We're just a bunch of drones. There's nothing to grab hold of – no cause, no purpose."

"It sounds like everyone around you has quit, too, but no one has left yet," Maddie said.

"Well, I can't afford to quit," Max said. "I've got bills to pay, responsibilities to meet. Besides, I do like some of the people still there. I mean, they're my friends. We've been through a lot together." Max unrolled his flatware from the paper napkin, and they clattered to the table.

"So then, it's the company?"

"A little," he said. "It's changed so much. There's a focus on making profit numbers and cutting costs, and nil on problem-solving or continuous improvement and learning to improve everyone. You know, all the stuff that drew me to it in the first place."

"What about your boss," she asked.

"Total jerk! They brought this one in from some other organization." Max rearranged the salt and pepper shakers to keep his hands busy. "No idea what his strengths are – and he has no idea about mine, either. He barely talks to anyone. When he does, it's a reprimand on why some stupid little task hasn't been done yet."

"Wow, sounds like you've got a bunch of issues to work through," she said.

"I'm a good person. Why is this happening to me?"

15

"Because you let it," she said.

Max ignored Maddie. "What happened to my job? The one I was comfortable in? The one I liked?"

"The only thing constant in life is change," Maddie said.

"Yeah, yeah, yeah. Cliché." Max waved her comment away while a waitress brought over their iced teas.

"If you don't believe me, crack open your old high school yearbook," she said. "Do you or anybody else look the same? Dress the same? Have the same hairstyle? Would you really want that?"

"No," Max shivered, "that would be pretty bad."

"Change is the only constant. If you think your job sucks but don't think you can quit, you have to figure out how to stay. Change it, and what you can't change, change your attitude about it. If you aren't going to leave it, you need to learn to love it…or at least tolerate it." she said.

"How do I do that?"

Maddie took a sip of her iced tea and then added a packet of sweetener. "Reflect, and determine if it's your job that has changed, or you. And what if neither changed? Would you be happy to keep doing what you're doing now for the next five years?"

"Hell no!"

"Then you better learn to recognize, respond, and thrive with change."

Max rolled his eyes. The waitress delivered their lunches; an oversized sandwich for Max and a salad for Maddie.

Determined, Maddie pressed on. "Maybe it's not too late; you might not be a complete wreck. Take a look outside your work. Is there anything making you happy?"

"I don't know." Max shrugged without giving it much thought.

"Some people go to the ballpark and do scream therapy. Others like to fish, or fix up an old car," she said.

"You know that's not really me."

"The point is to find something that has nothing to do with your present condition. You're looking for something different, a diversion that gets you up and going and gets you excited."

Maddie stabbed at her salad, and Max struggled to chew an ambitious bite of his sandwich.

"Yeah, it would be cool to feel excited or passionate about something," he said, "but what if it's too late? What if I've wrapped myself so tight around my work that the troubles there aren't allowing me to have fun or find peace in other areas of my life? What if I'm not happy anywhere?"

"Cripes! Give yourself a freaking break, would ya!" Maddie said, aggravated with Max's self-pity. "Listen to upbeat music or inspirational tapes or hang out with happy people. Remember, you want to feel better, right?"

"Yes."

She slapped her palm against the table. "Then get excited about it! Find your happy place, a peaceful spot, somewhere to contemplate life. Like Winnie the Pooh does in his thinking spot."

"How do I find it?" Max asked.

"Start to pay attention. Write down what makes you happy. Think back to what makes you laugh out loud. Keep a log or jot ideas down on sticky notes and refer to them to lift your spirits and learn a little about yourself."

After a while, their empty plates were cleared from the table, and Max and Maddie both sipped on refilled glasses of iced tea.

"If you think carefully and pay close attention, you'll find your happy place." Maddie said, "This place, or thing, will become a major touchstone for you. It's going to bring a smile to that sourpuss face of yours. You're going to do your daydreaming about this place. It will spur you into action and get you through the day. Your sanctuary may be as large as your home or as small as your favorite seat at a coffee shop. It might be a stretch of beach or a particular bench in the park."

Max looked up toward the ceiling and debated potential spots in his mind. "I see," he said.

"It might not be a concrete place for you. It might be time. Time spent with family and friends, or reading a book or painting. Either way, it'll fill a spot in your heart. You'll need to nurture it with strong love and appreciation," she said, "because it will most assuredly go away without your attention and protection. That prospect should scare you into some positive action if nothing else."

"That makes sense," Max admitted with a begrudged smile.

"So, you know what you have to do," Maddie said. "Know what your happy place is. There, you'll find a sense of peace, happiness, and excitement."

"Well, all that sounds great."

Maddie watched Max fidget with the discarded wrapper from his straw. "I have to caution you," she said. "Once you've identified your happy place and made it real, there will be an invasion. It's inevitable, so prepare for it."

"An invasion? That sounds ominous."

"It is. That's why you need to nurture it, to make it strong enough to defend itself in your absence. Build a fortress around it if you need to. Know that something will intrude on your time with your happy place, and it will probably come from work, making you hate work even more."

Max threw up his arms and sighed. "That's great."

"It is great because, at least by then, you'll have awakened some passion for defending it. So, see that; your work is good for something after all."

As they both stepped away from the table, ready to leave, Maddie turned to Max.

"Thanks for lunch," she said.

"Thank you for your time," he said.

"So, what three things do you need to do?" she asked.

Max stumbled for a moment, unprepared for a pop quiz. "Um…Acknowledge and honor change," he said.

Maddie held her finger up. "That's one."

"Find something or someplace that makes me happy."

"That's two," she said. "What's the third?"

"Defend and protect the place that makes me happy," he said.

"Good. Do those things, and you'll lay the groundwork for improvement," she said.

They exited the diner and stood out on the city sidewalk. "I know you well enough to know that you want to be part of something great," Maddie continued. "I'd like to share something my boss shared with me recently. She's not one for elaborate models or theories, so she was able to whittle this concept into a pretty simple model."

"Sock it to me," Max said.

"Group One are people who feel like others owe them something. They never seem to get enough. They consider it to be 'just a job,' so it doesn't matter anyway," Maddie explained.

"I know a few of them," Max said.

"If people feel that way, then that job has become a mismatch, and they should find something else. For various reasons, people in this group are of low value to the team. Not to be cruel, but they are *Greatness Inhibitors*."

"*Greatness Inhibitors*. Nice phrase," Max said with a smirk.

Maddie resumed her lesson.

"Group Two people don't love their job, but it pays the bills," she shrugged. "They wish things could be better and wonder how they could leverage what they are experiencing for what they want, which is to be helpful. They've had moments of greatness and liked how it felt."

"That sounds a bit like me," Max said.

"I think so, too," she said. "Following the model, you should place yourself where you can contribute most. Because right now you're of moderate value to the team, but you're a *Potential Star*."

Max winced at the assessment but could not find himself disagreeing. "Yeah, you're right."

"If you want to make a dramatic improvement, start hanging around Group Three, the people who see possibility," she said. "They're often the people who problem-solve away from work and have the sense that their professional life enriches a part of their personal life and visa versa. Begin to emulate them. They are rare and needed leaders. They're driven to continue to perform and enrich themselves and others. They are the highly valued 'Stars' in the organization."

Max turned to Maddie with a bright smile. "That one is you, right?" he asked.

Maddie blushed. "Partly… finally. It took a while to get there."

"I like it," he said. "You can tell where someone falls and what impact they could have on the organization."

"Well, you can tell a lot without exerting too much effort. But be careful using this; no one likes to be put in a box," she explained. "This is for a self-assessment or a way for a well-functioning team to have honest conversations about performance. Never use this to marginalize others or do something stupid like rank and yank, which is a heinous, autocratic, and antiquated strategy that most grown-ups who care about people would be embarrassed to use."

"Tell me how you really feel," Max chuckled.

"Nothing broadcasts that you don't value your employees like rank and yank," Maddie said. "Lousy leaders use it to create a fear-based, competitive, secretive, stressful, and cut-throat environment. It's short-term focused and ignores team dynamics. Modern and effective leaders know it's better to focus on employee development and growth rather than punitive measures. So, yeah, use the tool for self-reflection. I use it on myself as a sanity check to ensure I never become a *Greatness Inhibitor*."

"I couldn't imagine you inhibiting someone's greatness," Max smiled.

When you look in the mirror, describe who you see.

What do you think you sounded like to people who may have overheard your conversations today?

Is your job fun? Why or why not?

What's changed from the first day you started your job? *(Was it your job that changed, or you?)*

What if neither you nor your job changed? Would you be happy to keep doing what you're doing now for the next five years? *(If no, you must learn to recognize, respond and thrive with change.)*

Do you have a sense of purpose in what you do? Why or why not? *(If you do have a sense of purpose, what is it? Are you living on purpose?)*

List three things that currently make you happy.

1.

2.

3.

Figure out how to spend more time with the things and people that lift your spirits.

What or where is your 'happy place'?

WHO'S THE JERK?

The next day Max sat in morning traffic, agitated by the horns blasting around him. He glanced at his watch and tapped on the steering wheel.

Finally, inside his office building, Max sprinted toward a bank of elevators in the lobby.

"Hold the door!" he shouted.

Too late, the first door closed. He shuffled to the next and missed that one too. He looked at his watch again and heard a familiar ding. Behind him, another elevator door opened.

Max smiled and turned, only to see a slow-moving elderly couple working their way into the elevator with their young granddaughter. Max clenched his fist and regained composure as he followed close behind the threesome, hoping his presence would speed them along.

Once inside, he pushed the close button. The little girl pushed the open button. Max grimaced, looked around to see if anyone else was boarding, then pressed the close button again. The little girl pressed the open button again. The alarm buzzed.

The grandfather asked, "Do you remember which floor, dear?"

Max leaned on the close button. The buzzing stopped, and the elevator began to move. He pressed the number ten button.

"Two!" The granddaughter shouted.

"Good," said the grandfather.

The girl reached over and pressed the number two button. It illuminated, and her eyes sparkled. To Max's shock, she continued, pressing more buttons.

"Four, six, eight, nine, seven, five, three." she sang out.

The grandmother looked at the anguished expression on Max's face.

"Oh, dear. I'm sorry," she said.

The doors opened on the second floor, and the slow-moving threesome worked their way out. Max noticed the little girl had dropped her doll in the elevator. He kicked it out into the hall right as the doors closed.

Max bounded into a packed conference room. No available seats were left around the table, so he sat in a rickety chair along the wall. He scanned the room, attempting to catch his breath and catch up on a meeting that hadn't started yet. With concern, he listened in on one of the multiple conversations.

"I say they get rid of him. He brings no value to the team," said Gary.

"But he's a likable guy," said someone else.

"I don't care if he's likable. He can't pitch worth crap. He lost five of the last seven games," Gary replied.

Relieved, Max focused his attention on another end of the table.

"You're mistaken," Betty said.

"I'm not mistaken, I checked and rechecked several times, and I can never find them," Lois replies.

"Well, I can't buy into your theory; you're not looking hard enough," Betty said.

"I'm telling you they've stopped ordering the number two pencils. Mark my words; coffee will be the next thing to go," Lois said.

Max shook his head in disbelief. One of his coworkers was upset and being consoled by another.

"I still can't believe it," May said.

"He just walked right out?" Bev asks.

"He didn't say a word. He looked at me, turned his back, waited a minute, then raced out the door," Mary replied.

"He'll be back. He's done this to you before," Bev said. She gave Mary a reassuring rub on her shoulder.

"It's been three days already. He seemed so determined. I've never seen him so pissed."

"What do you suppose ticked him off?" Bev asked.

"Well, I switched from wet food to dry," Mary replied.

"Ohhh," Bev said with a hint of disappointment.

"It's supposed to help with the tartar build-up. I did it for him."

Max could not take anymore and stood. "Where is Fred? Wasn't there a meeting scheduled for this morning?"

The room went silent for a moment.

"He called in sick five minutes ago," Gary said. "Postponed it for tomorrow."

Max looked at his watch and shook his head. He left the conference room while the others resumed their discussions.

Max sat at a small round table in a coffee shop with Maddie. She attempted to contain herself from laughing.

"I'm surrounded by mediocrity. Like a dime in a pocketful of pennies," Max said.

"We all like to tell people how we've been wronged," Maddie said. "And we like to embellish it, so everyone knows our pain. It's the martyr syndrome."

"Maybe."

"Think about it. When you hear other people complain a lot, don't you think of all the alternatives they could have done to avoid their pain? And don't you think, even briefly, that they sound like a pathetic loser?"

"Of course I do," he chuckled.

"Well, surprise. They think the same of you," she said.

"I guess all the smart people have already left the company," he said.

"Maybe some of them have modified their attitudes to match their new circumstances," she offered.

"Maybe."

"Seriously, can you identify them?" she asked. "Are they in your circle? They need to be, so you had better find them quickly; otherwise, you are screwed. They could be the lifeline that stops you from sinking any further."

Max looked stone-faced at Maddie, then down at his empty cup. "I need more coffee."

Max stood in line and noticed the man before him struggling to get the correct change from his wallet. Max sighed repeatedly and then pushed past him with his cup the moment a second cashier arrived.

"Can I just get a refill, please?" he asked.

The man in line and both cashiers shot Max a dirty look. Nonetheless, soon his cup was filled to the brim. He turned back toward the table to rejoin Maddie. Someone mistakenly stepped in front of him, causing Max to spill hot coffee over his hands and onto his shoes. He sat down hard in his chair and started cleaning himself up.

"Do you see what I mean?" he said to Maddie. "See what I'm going through today? A bunch of idiots."

Maddie abruptly stopped giggling. "Believe it or not, people are generally good. Very few wake up each morning and commit to screwing you somehow. Oh, there may be a few for sure; and sometimes I can see why." She shot a look toward the cashier. "But in most cases, they're as disorganized and apathetic as you, so you should feel pretty safe."

"Thanks. Is that your version of tough love?"

"Listen, I'm going to share some advice with you because you're starting to act like a jerk." She leaned forward. "Beware the three donkey day."

"Okay, I'll bite," Max said as he finished wiping down his shoes and fingers with a napkin, crumpling it and throwing it onto the table. "What's that?"

"If you encounter three people who you feel are complete donkeys during your day, then you are probably being the ass. Go home and call it a day, or at least take a deep breath and keep your mouth shut before you make a bigger fool of yourself." Satisfied with making her point, she took a long sip from her cup.

They both sat quietly for a few minutes.

"You're right, Maddie," Max said, "I'm sorry. I'm just so burnt out–"

Maddie raised her hand and pitched forward again. "And don't blame it on burnout when you're the arsonist! When you moan and groan to the people putting up with you and all your crap and say you're feeling burnt out, it ticks them off because it's a load of garbage. As a human being, you can sustain a lot of real pain and hardship." Aggravated, she couldn't contain herself anymore and whacked the back of Max's head.

"Ouch!"

"You're blessed with a brain that has the ability to solve almost any problem set before it. You're being lazy. You don't want to hear it, but at its core, it's true."

"Well, it's still hard." Max sat back, rubbed his head, and sipped his cup.

"I know it's hard. Think of it like a box of leftover food in the refrigerator. You don't like what you see, but you need to do something with it. You've got choices. You can change it into something more palatable. You can choose to ignore it... for a little while, anyway. Or you can choose to get rid of it. Move on and find something else. The same applies to you and your job."

"I'm so frustrated. It's hard to get motivated to do anything."

"Listen, we are intrinsically motivated by one or more of three things. Personal growth and development, enhancing an important relationship, or working on something bigger than ourselves and leaving a legacy."

"I remember when I started my job," Max said, "I was excited and felt like I was finally able to make some changes and do important things."

Maddie turned hopeful. "Good."

"Then something came by and threw me off course. It even took away my desire to pursue those things anymore."

"Reflect and dig deep. Is there anything you can salvage?"

"I don't know," Max said.

"Why did you relinquish that control you had in your life?"

"I felt like I didn't have a choice," he said.

"But you did have a choice in your attitude and approach. And lately, your attitude has been... well, crappy."

Maddie sat back in her chair with her arms folded across her chest. Max sat, quiet, and thought for a moment.

"You've said a lot of things I need to think about. It's clear I need to get better control of my attitude, and surrounding myself with positive people is an obvious start."

"Each morning, it's up to you. You can wake up, drag yourself out of bed, look out the window, and say, "Good Lord, it's morning," or you can hop up, take a deep breath and say, "Good morning Lord.""

The next day the conference room was full of people again. This time, everyone looked attentively toward Mr. Seaver in front of the downward trending graph projected on the screen.

"So you see, if we don't focus on making the business more profitable, there won't be the opportunity to do the things that had drawn many of you into the company in the first place," Mr. Seaver said. "We've been doing some cutbacks on supplies, but we'll need to do much more than that going forward."

At lunchtime, Max sat on a bench with a sketchpad. His absentminded doodling began to form the shapes of nearby people, fountains, and birds. Suddenly, he was struck by a thought, which he jotted down in a nearby notebook with the phrase FRESH IDEAS written on the cover.

Later in the week, Max paced in his office. It was still cluttered, but now it felt like a productive war room. Flip charts covered with brainstormed notes, problem-solving tools, and words of inspiration filled the office. One of his lethargic coworkers, Gary, stepped into the office with a thin binder. Max grabbed it with excitement.

"Is this all of it?" Max asked.

"Um, yeah. That's what we could find right now," Gary said.

"I thought we agreed it would be done by today?" Max asked.

Gary shrugged and retreated out of the office. Max flipped through the skinny binder with disappointment, then tossed it on the desk with disgust. He paced around the office for a moment, mumbling to himself.

"Why can't they respond quicker? Am I unreasonable? Other people put unreasonable expectations on me all the time. I deliver."

Max picked up the phone and dialed a number.

"Hi, it's me. I'm due for another kick in the pants."

When was the last time you came across three 'donkeys'?

Reflecting back on that day, who was the biggest donkey? (If it wasn't you, you may want to think again or ask someone who was with you.)

Knowing what you now know, what will you do differently in the future?

What can you change?

What will you ignore?

What will you dispose of?

WHY AM I STILL HERE?

Max and Maddie sat at a corner table away from a group of skateboard-wielding high school kids who had swarmed the coffee shop in search of lattes and mochas.

"I don't know why people can't do what I tell them to do." Still livid, Max vented to Maddie. "It's like they have the memory of goldfish. After three minutes, they have no recollection of what their task was."

Maddie sighed. "You should be convinced by now that if you continue to behave the same way you've been acting, you will build momentum and speed toward a much-deserved outcome. Unfortunately for you, that outcome will probably not be positive."

"I thought I was doing better," Max said. "I feel doomed." He lifted his cup of coffee and took a sip. He burned the tip of his tongue again.

"You're not doomed, but you need to change your approach toward the people you work with," Maddie said. "It doesn't have to be complicated. Be a servant leader and ask others, "What one thing can I do for you that will most help you make a positive difference?"

"Why do I want to ask that?"

"Because you owe your coworkers more than you've been giving them," she said.

Max grimaced. "I suppose."

"I'm going to ask you a series of questions; try to answer them for yourself first, then your team. By asking them, you'll create a positive and proactive buzz. Then, with that newfound energy, you can direct the momentum. It's your leadership – not your management, that's crucial."

Max pulled a pen from his portfolio and set it against his yellow-lined paper tablet. "I'm ready."

"First, ask, 'Why are you still here?' Keep probing until one or more of the three intrinsic motivators are revealed. For personal development, because of enriching experiences with others; or to work on leaving a legacy."

Max looked over what he had written. "Why are you still here? That could be a revealing question."

Maddie popped her eyebrows up and grinned. "Second, define your primary learning style. Is it *Action-Oriented*? Are you likely to roll up your sleeves and get to it, preferring to learn through trial and error? Are you *People-Oriented*? Do you like to confer with others who may have experienced the problem before you? Or are you *Information-Oriented*? Are you the first to look for the training manual or documentation you can refer to frequently?"

"Well, I'm an information learner," Max said. "Heck, I read the toothpaste tube."

Maddie chuckled. "The third thing is to recognize that in any organization, you must be successful in three areas: Customer Satisfaction, Employee Satisfaction, and Profitable Revenue Growth. These are the three legs of the stool that you are resting your career on. If the stool is wobbling, fix a leg before you fall off. Which areas do you feel you could make the greatest positive impact?"

"That's going to require some thought," Max said. "At first, I was going to say all of them. But if the goal is to make the greatest contribution, it may be best to focus on one to start."

"Exactly," she nodded. "Fourth, review all your choices and ask, 'What will I do in the next week to get started?' Find linkages and hold yourself to your commitments."

"Maddie," he remarked, "you seem so pulled together. I almost hate you."

She laughed. "I hope not. But do you remember, about a year and a half ago, when I was ready to pull my hair out? I became withdrawn, staying away from people?"

"Yeah, I remember now. I thought you had fallen off the face of the earth."

"Well, luckily, I started working with some great folks who didn't allow me to stray too far. My boss helped too. She shared a lot of what I'm sharing with you."

"So there is hope," he said.

"Yes, there is hope. It's not instant, but it does get better."

Max flipped through the pages of his notepad and straightened up in his chair. "Let me tell you what I jotted down to ensure I got it all."

"Good idea."

"First, ask, 'Why are you still here?' and keep probing until I discover the reasons, which could be: For personal development, because of enriching experiences with others, or to work on leaving a legacy."

"Yes, good," she said.

"Second, find my primary learning style; Action-Oriented, People-Oriented, or Information-Oriented."

"Perfect."

"Third, in any organization, you need to be equally successful in Customer Satisfaction, Employee Satisfaction, and Profitable Revenue Growth, so determine in which areas I could make the greatest positive impact."

"Correct," she said.

"Then fourth, identify what I will do in the next week to get started?"

"You got it. But you know what? This is a crisis, so move faster. Instead of a week, figure out what you can do in the next day."

"A day?" Max took a deep breath. "I'll give it a shot."

"Remember, be open to the answers. Don't ask people what you can do to help, and then try to squirm out of it when they tell you. That's a trust killer. Make it your mission to complete the requests that anyone was brave enough to share with you."

Max sat at his desk in his office when a loud jingle from his cell phone jarred him away from the computer screen. He looked at it and saw that it was Maddie calling. For some reason, he stood to take her call.

"Good morning Maddie," he said.

"Okay, I've been thinking. I've shared many thoughts and concepts with you, but it's unclear if you've actually begun to use them to improve yourself. I'll assume you have. But you must know; important change will not occur with halfhearted attempts. It takes true commitment. That means doing it even if it's hard or you don't feel like it."

"Maddie," he tried to interrupt.

"Wait, this is important. You need to know it's about more than you. Because of your position as a leader, how you feel can affect others, and the moment you start to affect the lives of other people negatively is when I start to get pissed off. The world is filled with enough poor leaders. You must keep your commitments to others at all costs."

Max tried to interject again. "Maddie."

"Let me finish. This is about responsibility and applies to anyone who has formal or informal influence over a team of people. As a leader, people depend on you. Anyone you come in contact with – you affect or influence in some way. If you are not totally and completely there, negative outside influences will get to them. It will fester, resentment will grow, and that would be catastrophic."

"Yes, it would be," he said.

"Don't let that happen. Protect your people. Just because you're a basket case doesn't mean innocent people should suffer. Focus on improving their jobs, their outlook, and even their life. If you're lucky, you'll feel better about yourself too. If not, well, at least you're not dragging everyone else down."

Max sat back in his chair and gazed out the window. A smile formed across his face.

"Maddie, thanks for caring enough to call. I got it. If nothing else, I should focus on improving other people's jobs, outlook, and lives."

"Yes," she said. "I'm concerned you've become apathetic and have adopted the 'so what, I don't care, what difference does it make?' attitude. That might be one of your biggest problems. You must find something to start to care about. You've got to get over yourself and realize that you can still make a difference. In fact, it's your responsibility to make a positive difference."

They were both silent for a long moment.

"You've gotten less diplomatic with me over these last few weeks," he joked.

"I want to be clear," she said. "It's not about you. It's about them. You need to summon your courage. When something is wrong, and you know it's wrong, or there is a direct or indirect assault on your values, beliefs, mission, goals, or people, you need to fight back. Get an exception to the policy. Break a rule. Do what is right, even if it's not correct. Take a stand. Make a difference. Lobby for change. Run to things – not away from them. Operate from a position of strength, not weakness. You are better than the problem that is set before you. If you're still talking with me after everything I've said, you must still care and want to make a difference."

"I do," he said. "I do care and want to make a difference."

"Good for you! Now, can you define what? Try hard. Something is spurring you on. There's a vision deep in there, aching to be realized. Go breathe some new life into it."

After saying goodbye, Max hung up the telephone, tossed it on his desk, and let out a deep breath. Agitated, he stood behind his chair and clutched the back of it. He knew it would be hard work to improve his outlook, but he thought he was improving. He had been beaten down, ignored, and frustrated for so long. There was no way he would be able to change with a flick of a switch. He probably has been less ignored than misunderstood, and the person beating Max down the most was himself. He bowed his head for a moment and then lifted it again. He folded his arms in front of him and wandered toward the entrance of his office. He leaned against the doorframe and looked out toward the cubicles that caged his team members. His face became ashen again when he realized how poor of a leader he had been to them lately.

Late that afternoon, Max went outside for a walk around the block. He felt downtrodden, and it showed across his face. His shoulders sloped forward, and each step he took seemed like a burden to his feet. Lost in thought, he rounded a corner and ran into the ever-radiant Maddie.

"Oh, my gosh, what happened? You look miserable," she said.

"I feel like I've been a horrible teammate and a worse leader. I'm not getting what I want," he said.

"I didn't mean to beat you up so bad," Maddie said. "I just wanted to rattle your cage."

"It wasn't all you," Max said.

"Hey, it's not too late," she said. "You can change it – for yourself and others. Start to act as if. When people ask, 'How are you?' – don't mumble, 'fine.' When they ask, 'Can I do anything to help?'– don't say 'no .' Seek, and ye shall find, ask, and ye shall receive."

Max nodded in dejected agreement. "I just want to feel better," he said.

Maddie grabbed his arm to console him. "Sweetie, very little will drop in your lap. Come to think of it, what things normally drop in people's laps?"

Max shrugged his shoulders. "I dunno, crumbs and spilled drinks."

"Well, no one wants that! You need to forcefully, calmly, and professionally tell people what you need so that you can do your job. Let them know if they can't provide, neither can you."

Max cracked a weak smile. "It's true."

"You know, it may also be time to start looking for something new. Tap the network. Ask for help. People like helping people reach their goals."

"That's another whole arena. You assume I know what my goals are."

"They're easy to find. What things do you do at work that you enjoy? Working with people? Creating presentations? Analyzing data? Every time you find that hint of passion, pay attention to yourself and see how you respond. When it feels great, enjoy it. Relish it and do everything you can to repeat it. Spend more time doing that. Ignore the rest if you can afford to. It's the passion-inducing moments that give you happiness and personal success. People follow passionate and competent leaders, so keep working on your skills and strengths."

"You make everything sound so easy," Max sighed.

"They're simple. Not easy," she said. "I'm not letting you get lazy on me. Know your strengths. Dig up any personal assessments or ask five people you interact with daily what they think your strengths are. Look for the repeated positive themes and begin to do those things. Refine your strengths. Let all the other things atrophy. You weren't built to do them anyway, so don't worry about them."

Maddie dug through her purse and pulled out a small light blue booklet.

"Here, take this. I have more at home," she said.

"What is it?" Max asked.

"It's called a 'Disposable Journal'. You use it for a week. Each day there's a prompt, and you journal your response for twenty minutes. At the end of the week, you throw out everything but the last page."

"Seems like a waste."

"I know, but it's not. It works. It's based on therapeutic writing. You write out your problems and then let them go."

"Like magic," Max joked.

Maddie frowned at him. "It's not magic. It takes work. But call it magic if that makes you feel better. Try it for a week, and then let's meet for coffee."

She hugged Max, and he returned to his office, his mind filled with thoughts of things he needed to release. He flipped through the pages of the small journal and committed himself to sit with it for seven days.

Seven Days of Prompting

Day One - Think and then get it out.

What's troubling you right now? Is it a fear? Are you angry or perhaps sad? Today, put it out there. Think of this journal as your trusted friend whom you've not seen in a while. What do you want to tell it?

Day Two - What's going on with you?

Today, describe your current state. What are your thoughts and feelings? Who's to blame, and why do you feel that way? Put it out there and write for a solid twenty minutes.

Day Three - What do you call it?

Today, list several words and phrases that describe how you feel. Circle a few of them; connect any similar words or phrases with arrows. Put a star next to one or two that really speak to you. If the words escape you, draw a picture.

Day Four - Isolate the pain.

Today, pick one of those words or phrases that you starred yesterday. Focus on it and explicitly describe it using all your senses. What does it look like to you? How does it smell, taste, and sound? How do you feel around it? Thoroughly examine it for twenty minutes.

Day Five - Get physical.

Today, think about what's been holding you back and describe how you physically feel inside and out. What's happening to your hands and legs? How does your stomach feel? How about your face and head? What are your lips and eyes doing? What else have you noticed? Write it out.

Day Six - Letter it out.

Today, draft a letter to the person or persons that have had their grip on you. Detail how you feel and what must change. If you can forgive them, do so. If not, just describe how you will be better with this "thing" behind you.

Day Seven - What now?

Today, write a letter to your future self. You have bared your soul and learned a lot. Congratulations! Now use the good feelings to encourage yourself. Write out new goals. Consider framing them with these questions. How much and by when? Why? Who can help? Be action-oriented.

Ask yourself, "Why am I still here?" Keep probing until one or more of the three intrinsic motivators are revealed;

- ☐ Personal growth and development
- ☐ Enhancing important relationships
- ☐ Working on something bigger than yourself and leaving a legacy

What is your primary learning style?

- ☐ Are you *Action-Oriented*? Are you likely to roll up your sleeves and take action, preferring to learn through trial and error?
- ☐ Are you *People-Oriented*? Do you like to confer with others who may have experienced the problem prior to you?
- ☐ Are you *Information-Oriented*? Are you among the first to look for the training manual or some type of reference documentation?

In which of these areas do you feel you could make the greatest positive impact;

- ☐ Customer Satisfaction,
- ☐ Employee Satisfaction,
- ☐ Profitable Revenue Growth?

Review all the choices that you made and answer the question, "What am I going to do tomorrow to get started?"

Write down or draw your vision or picture of success.

Use the prompts from the Disposable Journal to write it out and let it go.

You can order your own physical Disposable Journal at https://disposablejournal.com/

LAME EXCUSES AND FOUR MUSTS

Max and Maddie sat in their familiar seats in the coffee shop. Max was more pulled together, but he still looked weary around his eyes.

"The Disposable Journal you gave me was helpful this past week," he said. "I've become determined to start protecting my people, to improve their jobs, outlook, and lives," he said. "I've found it easier to do this by running to things and not away from them. I know it's better to make decisions from a position of strength. Overall, I'm making good progress, but some things have not changed. I'm trying to figure out what to do about them in the meantime."

"While the network is working, you need to too," Maddie said. "The fish don't always bite; the ball doesn't always go through the hoop. What's going on in your work world that you can use – before it goes away?"

Max's face remained blank as he tried to decipher what Maddie said. She noticed his confusion.

"Act like the boy who walked into a room full of horse manure. While his father grimaced and plugged his nose, the boy excitedly proclaimed, 'There's got to be a pony in here somewhere,' she said.

"That's a kid who knows what he's looking for."

"Get optimistic and find the upside of everything. Make a game of it. A boring training class becomes a test of endurance. Got a thick new policy manual to go through? Time to practice your speed-reading. Become the problem solver and measure your progress. Keep a log of the problems you solve each day. Track and improve your average."

Max's eyes brightened. "I could do that."

"Take it from me; you have to find a balance. You need to make time for yourself. Take a break from the madness. If you can get away for a while, great, even for an afternoon or a lunch hour. Slip away from your job and work on something else. Anything. Make the best grocery list the world has ever seen. Wax your car. Clean your closet. Play. Buy a set of Lego Bricks and build something. Make sure you're active and engaging as many of your senses as possible. Sitting on the couch with a pint of ice cream, watching reruns of "Friends" does not count. You need to move your mind, body, and heart. And when you're done, there needs to be something you can look at with a feeling of accomplishment and satisfaction."

"That reminds me of the story of the Starfish Thrower," Max said.

Maddie smiled, and Max was sure she had heard the story, but he told it anyway. "An old guy, who's been cranky like me, walks along a beach after a storm. In the distance, he notices a young girl heaving objects back into the surf. As the man gets closer to her, he calls out, 'What are you doing?' The girl replies, 'I'm helping these starfish get back home.' The man looks around and, for the first time, notices hundreds upon hundreds of starfish washed up on the shore. He shakes his head, 'Look at how many there are. You can't possibly make a difference!' Without stopping, the girl reaches for another stranded starfish and throws it back to the ocean, 'I made a difference to that one,' she said as she reached for another." Max sighed. "I know I have to do something."

Maddie nodded. "Take an inventory of your life. Are you in harmony? Do you have everything you need and want? Is it all readily available, or do you have to do something different or go someplace else to find it?"

"Good questions," Max said.

"You've gotten comfortable with all your complaining. People seem to be giving you pity – and you've been playing a great victim.

Keep it up, and you could keep doing what you've been doing until you retire or die, whichever comes first."

"That's a dismal choice," he said.

"Yes, it is," she said. "You know that the best and sweetest fruit is out on the limb. So, figure out how you are going to get it. You can wait until it drops – overripe, maybe worm-ridden. You can try to knock it down, but that can result in bruising. Or you can climb the tree and reach for it."

"There's risk in all of the choices," he said.

"Welcome to life. Now start living," Maddie smiled.

They walked a few steps, and Max's grimace faded. Maddie grabbed his arm.

"How about spending some time working on you?" she asked. "What do you want to do with yourself? You've got to have a clue. Reach back into your childhood if you need to. What did you want to be when you grew up? Why? Examine that in today's context. Is it still appealing? If not, why not? If yes, then why the heck aren't you doing it now?"

Max pondered the question while Maddie continued. "Go ahead; list your ten best excuses. Write them down and then prioritize them, one through ten, like you would your goals. Go after the top three and back-solve them; examine why they exist. Get rid of the barriers. Those SOBs are keeping you from your dream."

Feelings of overwhelm dampened Max's excitement. "So what do I do first?" he asked.

"List your excuses," she said. "Think of yourself as an actor on a television show, hired to play a role. You work on your craft and contribute toward getting high weekly ratings, so the show avoids cancellation, and you get renewed each season. You perform in a way that leads to the show's success, and you eventually earn awards and recognition and offers to play even bigger roles. Remember, you want to be a 'highly valued star,' not a 'greatness inhibitor.'"

Several weeks later, Max and Maddie greeted each other with a hug and a peck on the cheek. Max carried himself differently than before. His sloping shoulders had been replaced with the stance of a confident person of action. His eyes were wide open instead of weary, and an easy smile crossed his face.

"Oh, sweetie, you look great," Maddie said with delight.

"Even though some of it was painful, a lot of your advice has been right on target, and I'm determined to prove that I've been listening to all of your guidance," Max said with a twinkle in his eye. "The first thing I needed to do was acknowledge and honor the change around me. I had to figure out how to deal with it and learn how to be happy again. Once I identified that I had to be prepared to defend and protect the things that make me happy."

"Good for you," Maddie said.

"I also needed to beware of the three donkey days I was having. I learned that it was foolish to blame what I was going through on burnout when I was acting like an arsonist. I had a choice. I could change, ignore things for a little while, or move on, but I had to do something," he said. "I rediscovered what motivates me and remembered how I felt when I first got this job and why I wanted it to begin with. And that it was up to me to choose my attitude and approach."

"Did I say all that?" Maddie blushed.

"You did indeed," Max said.

She giggled and sipped her drink. "I am good."

"I needed to become less selfish, so I began asking people, 'What one thing can I do for you that will most help you make a positive difference?' I was amazed at the responses. It caused some people to pause and think – and they appreciated the help. If I found people were being negative, I challenged them and asked them why they were still doing what they were doing."

"People like feeling useful, and that comes with helping others," Maddie said. "You help them, and by doing that, they help you."

"I figured out my learning style and began to identify where I and others could begin to make the most positive impact, either in customer satisfaction, employee satisfaction, or profitable revenue growth. I knew talking about it was a good start, but I needed more. So, I built weekly action plans around each goal."

"It's crucial to set goals with measurements and timelines. Accomplishing them without that is more luck than effort," Maddie said.

Max nodded and continued. "I learned that I needed to protect my people at all costs and improve their jobs, outlook, and livelihood are some of my key roles. I've learned to begin to run to things – not away from things. In the past, if I heard someone grumbling and heading down the wrong path, I would shrug. Now I run to those opportunities and find the teachable moments. I step in, clarify their assumptions, and redirect them down a more informed path. It's been strengthening my relationships."

A smile crossed Maddie's face. "If people don't have the right facts, they make them up, so it makes better sense for them. When you give them the facts, they more often reach the same conclusion you do and will be more likely to support you."

"I also used to spend time dwelling on what I was missing, what I didn't know. I used to undermine myself. I now understand that it's always better to operate from a position of strength, not weakness, as I continue to refine my vision. People like to follow others who are passionate and competent, and because of that, I continue to refine my strengths. By making my strengths stronger, I neutralize, or at least minimize my weaknesses."

Maddie beamed. "It's amazing how far you've come."

"It wasn't easy. I had to consciously become optimistic and turn everything into an upside. I trained myself to find the pony in almost every situation. It helped to list my ten best excuses for not doing something, to see how foolish I was acting."

Maddie was giddy, and her infectious enthusiasm rubbed off on Max. "I think you're ready," she said.

"Ready for what?" he asked.

"To help others get out of the dumps and to start building a successful organization. I want to tell you about 'The Four Musts.'"

Intrigued, Max asked, "What are those?"

"A guy I worked with shared them with me – although they can be hard to accomplish and require regular fine-tuning, they're sound and make a lot of sense to me. I use them to help me guide my team. It also helps me lead forward."

"Well, what are you waiting for – lay them on me!" Max said.

"There must be a strong leader and strong, pervasive leadership," Maddie said. "Charisma is not leadership, although it can be a helpful tool to gain an audience's acceptance quickly. Effective leaders share a passion for and a record of accomplishments. A person or a group of people, who are honest, forthright, markedly visible, and approachable, demonstrate strong leadership daily. Leaders fulfill their insatiable need to be out in the field regularly. When not walking on the front lines, they talk with people who work there in town hall-style meetings and one-on-one. They remember that just as the shepherd is there for the benefit of the flock, leadership is there to serve the people, and they take that responsibility seriously."

Max nodded. "It's one thing to talk like a leader, quite another to act like one," he said.

"Exactly. The organization must also have a repeatable, compelling vision and a sense of purpose. It should be a clear and concise singular vision. Every activity that the organization tackles must be able to foster a closer linkage to that compelling vision. It must be memorable and repeatable so that every message, action, and strategy supports the purpose within their obvious connections. The clarity of the vision should be worded and promoted so that others can understand it, support it, be excited by it, grow some passion around it, and be inventive in discovering new ways to achieve that purpose."

"Too often people spend too much time and energy trying to create a literary masterpiece instead of a clear, easy-to-follow, and understandable vision," Max said.

"It's a terrible waste of resources," Maddie said. "Leadership is about inspiring people and waking them up, not tiring people and putting them to sleep. There must be a sense of overwhelming optimism. The compelling vision is not only the day-to-day, here's what we need to do and why, but is also the overarching, here is our place on earth, our legacy, and the good we wish to do. Living that is what creates a legacy. Knowing that is what helps create positivism. That positive approach has to be all-encompassing. Tolerance of rampant apathy or negativism is a weakness. If optimism is not visible, alarms should sound, and priority should be given to overcoming the obstruction. This doesn't forego the crucial role of devil's advocate and challenging viewpoints - but to leave negative remarks or feelings unchecked, even in the simplest day-to-day transactions, is to enable the contagion. Counter the virus with positive encouragement and recognition."

Max smiled. "You don't want to be Pollyanna with everything; that can be as dangerous. But negativity is an acid that corrodes everything," he said.

"It must be neutralized," she said.

"What's the fourth must?" he asked.

"There must be a regular diet of meaningful recognition. Positive reinforcement, thanks, and praise are the nutritional components of a healthy workforce, the helium that lifts the organizational balloon to new heights. It is a currency that many organizations are afraid of spending, yet, its value can be limitless. Without it, or withholding it until the perfect moment, can result in, at worst, a bankruptcy of human potential and, at best, leave people with a feeling of emotional deficiency. All people want to do a good job, regardless of which motivations they declare to be driven by; the rewards of learning new experiences, enhancing important relationships, or legacy building. People will reward those who notice what they have already contributed with even greater performance."

Max nodded again. "It's amazing. People often think about thanking people for a job well done – but thinking it is not the same as doing it."

"The best of intentions are still only intentions. To make an impact, you must actually do something."

"Well, I finally feel ready," Max said.

"It's great to see the transformation you've made. I'm so proud of you."

"I could not have done any of it without you. You opened my eyes and forced me to take the focus off my problems and instead put energy toward my potential. Thanks so much."

"Don't be silly. That's what friends - and leaders - do for each other."

What did you do that moved your mind, body, and heart?

Take an inventory of what it is you want. Is it readily available, or do you have to go someplace else for it? Would you?

What did you want to be when you grew up? Why?

Now examine your answer in today's context. Is it still appealing? If not, why not? If yes, then why the heck aren't you doing it now?

Go ahead; list your ten best excuses for not doing it.

1.

2.

3.

4.

5.

6.

7.

8.

9.

10.

Do you have a passion for a record of accomplishment? What are your top three accomplishments right now?

1.

2.

3.

How often do you talk to people who are on the front lines?

Does your organization have a repeatable compelling vision and sense of purpose?

If it does, what is it?

Does it excite you or anyone else?

How do you handle apathy or negativism when you encounter it?

What more could you do?

THE FOUR MUSTS

1. Are you a strong leader, and do you provide strong, pervasive leadership?

2. Do you have a repeatable, compelling vision and sense of purpose?

3. Do you have a sense of overwhelming optimism?

4. Do you provide a regular diet of meaningful recognition?

FINAL THOUGHTS

Everyone hits a brick wall from time to time, and it's easy to quit. The problem is – too many people quit because it's easy. This story offered a series of suggestions on how to stay when you want to quit. If you skipped over the reflections at the end of each chapter, go back and give them some thought. They're there to help you to get over yourself.

Now it's up to you. It's time to put yourself back in the driver's seat of your career and your life and begin pursuing the dreams, hopes, and aspirations that you've been moaning about all this time. People believe in you. Now believe in yourself.

ABOUT THE AUTHOR

Karl Bimshas is a Leadership Advisor and prolific author. Boston-bred and California-chilled, he earned an M.S. in Executive Leadership from the University of San Diego and a B.A. in Mass Communications from Emerson College. He has held several operational and sales positions in public and private corporations.

Learn more at www.KarlBimshasConsulting.com